D1273605

PLAY THE GAME

KARATE

KARL OLDGATE

BLANDFORD

First published 1990 by
Ward Lock and revised by Blandford 1993,
Villiers House, 41-47 Strand, London, WC2N 5JE.

Reprinted 1993, 1994

A Cassell imprint.

Designed by Anita Ruddell
Illustrations by Bob Williams

Text set in Helvetica
by August Filmsetting, Haydock, St Helens.
Printed and bound in Great Britain
by The Bath Press, Avon

British Library Cataloguing in Publication Data
Oldgate, Karl

Karate.—(Play the game)
1. Karate
I. Title   II. Series
796.8'153

ISBN 0 7137 24102

Acknowledgements

The publishers wish to thank Sylvio Dokov for
supplying all the photographs in this book.

Frontispiece: **Paul Alderson in action,
rumoured to be considering early
retirement but one of England's greatest
new names in karate.**

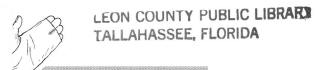

CONTENTS

FOREWORD

Play the Game: Karate gives the newcomer to karate a clear and broad insight into this exciting sport. It explains the history and development of karate and gives a comprehensive picture of how it is practised today. Karate has recently been approved as an Olympic sport, which reflects its position as one of the fastest-growing sports in the world at present.

The author has presented his work in a form attractive and understandable to the novice. In particular, his explanation of traditional karate practice and his translation of the phraseology are quite thorough and will help the new student to pick up the 'extras' which always accompany the learning of this sport.

Karate is not easy to learn. It requires concentration and hard work. But for anyone who is prepared to make the effort, the results can be surprising. Many people who thought they had no aptitude for karate have found that they have become proficient; and they enjoy the fitness and comradeship which comes from being a member of a karate club.

I recommend this book as a useful accompaniment to the practical training in a club approved by the official governing body of Karate.

Barney Whelan
Chairman, British Karate Federation
Chairman, Martial Arts Commission
Chairman, Scottish Karate Board of Control
Member, World Union of Karate Organisations
Member, European Karate Union

HISTORY & DEVELOPMENT OF KARATE

Karate, which literally means 'empty hand', comes in many different forms as you will see when you read through this book. But it all stems from the 5th century AD and a Zen Buddhist priest called Bhodidharma.

In those days priests were experts at self-defence because they were constantly battling (literally!) against parishioners of differing faiths. Their self-defence was based on yoga techniques.

Towards the end of the 5th century Bhodidharma went from India to China to teach at the Shaolin-Szu monastery where he taught his pupils the yoga techniques necessary to bring together the enlightenment of both body and soul. However, he found the exercise too strenuous for his students, and in an effort to build up their stamina he introduced a form of Chinese fighting called *kempo* into their training schedule. It worked, and soon the Shaolin-Szu Temple became one of the most respected fighting schools in China.

Kempo was used alongside medicine techniques of the day and various vital parts of the body were pinpointed for medical science which the Chinese used in acupuncture. These target areas were used as areas of attack in *kempo* and later formed the basis for attack areas of karate.

Although the Shaolin-Szu techniques soon spread throughout China, it was being practised with local variations of the basic technique in various parts of the country. The techniques were soon carried to neighbouring countries and across waters to nearby islands. One such island to benefit from the Shaolin-Szu style of combat was Okinawa, the main island in the Ryukyu chain which stretches from Japan to Taiwan.

Okinawa had already had its own form of combat for many years before the arrival of the Shaolin-Szu technique. It was known simply as *te* which meant hand and was a form of unarmed combat which made full use of the hands.

Te had fallen into disuse as warriors started carrying weapons. But in the late 15th century the *te* form of fighting received a boost when restrictions on the use and carrying of arms were imposed on Okinawa's residents. When *kempo* reached Okinawa, the Japanese own style of fighting (*te*) combined with the Chinese form to create *Tang Hand*.

Shotokan is the most popular style of karate practised in Britain, with more than 20,000 exponents. It is the form of karate that deals with basic traditions and training within a formal, disciplined environment, and is the one we will be looking at more closely later in the book.

As for the other styles, *shitoryu* was founded by Kenwa Mabuni who took his style to Japan in 1930. Chojun Miyagi, like Mabuni and Funakoshi, hailed from Okinawa, and took his style *gojuryu* to Japan. Although born in Okinawa he lived in China for many years and studied *kempo*. He was an expert at 'in-fighting'.

Hironori Ohtsuka was a Japanese student of *ju-jitsu* at Waseda University, and adopted karate techniques of *ju-jitsu* to form the *wadoryu* (Way of Peace) school of karate. Another Japanese student, Chojiro Tani founded the *shukokai* (Way for All) school which emphasizes speed and movement. A former student of Mabuni, he broke away to form his own school in 1950.

The final major style of karate is *kyokushinkai* (The Peak of Truth) which was founded by the Korean, Masutatsu Oyama. As a 15-year-old in 1938 he went to Japan to study aviation. To strengthen his self-discipline he lived a life of solitude in the mountains for two years and is reported to have once fought 52 bulls unarmed!

There are other techniques, like *wadokai, gojukai, shotokai, kanshinryu,* and the Chinese *kung-fu* kicking and punching form which was popularized by actor Bruce Lee. Wing-chun was another system used by Lee. But the five schools as outlined are the ones regarded as the principle styles of karate.

Because each style was at first unique, the possibility of competition between rival exponents is impossible, and indeed unthinkable. Their style and techniques are so

However, the word karate was only eventually adopted in the 20th century. In 1922 (Gichin) Funakoshi, an Okinawan exponent of *Tang Hand*, was invited to give a demonstration in Japan. He had combined some of the skills of *te*, *Tang Hand* and the Japanese *Ju-jitsu* to create a new form of fighting. Funakoshi called the new form 'karate' and wrote: 'As a mirror's polished surface reflects whatever stands before it and a quiet valley carries even small sounds, so must the student of karate render his mind empty of selfishness in an effort to react appropriately towards anything he might encounter.' This is the meaning of **kara** in karate and remains one of the principle concepts; the emptying of the mind of all thoughts.

Funakoshi therefore allied the new form of combat to that of Zen Buddhism of the 5th century. Zen was the meditation aspect of karate, while karate was the action element.

Funakoshi's style of karate was known as *Shotokan* (so named because his nickname was Shoto) and it was to be the forerunner of other styles which developed – *shitoryu, gojuryu, wadoryu, shukokai,* and *kyokushinkai.*

Tsuguo Sakumoto of Japan has been one of the world's most outstanding Kata experts in recent years.

individual that respective schools take all precautions to make sure 'outsiders' can't get a look at their training schedules (*katas*).

Because of the high level of European and American servicemen in Japan during the last war, many became fans of one form or another of karate and some took what they had learnt back to their respective countries. It helped to spread the karate word worldwide but there still remained so many different styles that international competition was impossible. However, in 1964, in an effort to formulate a standardized set of rules, the Federation of All Japan Karate-do Organization (FAJKO) was formed with state approval. But progress was slow and it was not until 1970, when other national associations had started springing up, that the first 'all styles' world championship was organized and held in Tokyo. At the same time a meeting was held and a world governing body, the World Union of Karate-do Organizations, was established.

The British association had been established in 1967 and when they went to Paris for the second world championship in 1972 they became the first country to beat Japan in international competition. Since then, Great Britain has become one of the world's leading karate nations with fighters like Vic Charles, Jeoff Thompson, Pat Mackay and Jim Collins winning world individual titles.

EQUIPMENT & TERMINOLOGY

(While it is fully appreciated that many women and girls participate in karate, for simplicity all references to karateka *are in the male form. This isn't chauvinism... just a case of making the job a bit easier!)*

Before learning how to practise karate, it is important to familiarize yourself with the equipment needed, and the terminology you will come across as you get to grips with the game.

EQUIPMENT

Geting started in karate is not all that expensive. You can start by wearing a track suit, which you will probably have anyway. But if you want to buy a karate suit (*karategi*) then it will cost anything between £20 and £50.

The suit is white and light-fitting like a judo suit. It should not have any coloured piping or identification marks on it. The jacket must be long enough to cover the hips. Women may wear a plain white T-shirt under their jacket. The sleeves of the jacket must come at least half way down the forearm, and the trouser legs must cover at least two-thirds of the shin. To prevent perspiration dripping into your eyes a head band (*hachimaki*) can be worn, but not in a

kumite (contest). Like judo, shoes are not worn when performing a kata or in a competitive contest.

The jacket of the suit is tied with a belt which, like other martial arts, is of varying colour depending upon a fighter's level of skill. The belt system varies according to karate style but all styles have Kyu (student) and Dan (senior) grades. The following is an example of a typical belt grading system, starting with the least experienced to most experienced of fighters:

Novice – white
6th Kyu – red
5th Kyu – yellow
4th Kyu – orange
3rd Kyu – green
2nd Kyu – blue
1st Kyu – brown
1st–10th Dan – black

All Dans are black belts and it is very rare to find a fighter of a higher grade than 6th Dan. If a fighter attains 8th Dan status he has the option to wear a red belt which shows he has completed his full circle of learning from 6th Kyu to 6th Dan.

During competitive bouts one fighter wears a red belt and is referred to as *aka*. The other wears a white belt and he is referred to as *shiro*. Each must also wear an identifying number on their backs.

The fully attired karateka *in his* karategi
and wearing regulation mitts.

EQUIPMENT · & · TERMINOLOGY

You are not allowed to roll up the sleeves of your jacket or the legs of your trousers, and you must not wear a dirty *karategi*.

For protection, white protective padded mitts are worn. They must have no more than 1cm ($\frac{3}{8}$in) of padding and have an uncovered thumb. While karate in the modern-day form is sporting-based and is not intended to cause harm to its participants, accidents can happen and the wearing of these mitts helps reduce the risk of such accidents .

Gumshields are also recommended and, for the men, a well-fitting jockstrap is also suggested as a vital piece of your karate attire.

The only other expense you will incur will be in joining a club and/or paying for lessons. Membership fees vary according to the club and can be anything from between £5 and £25. Lessons, which normally last between 1 and 2 hours, will cost anything from £1 to £5. But it is all money well spent for a sport that you will get a lot of pleasure from.

Because most karate practise does not involve throws, the fighting area does not need to be as padded as that for judo. In fact, an area as heavily padded as a judo mat would slow down a karate fighter. The mats should be of a non-slip type and have a low friction value on the upper surface.

The regulation mitt.
Dirty, torn or frayed mitts are not allowed in tournament events.

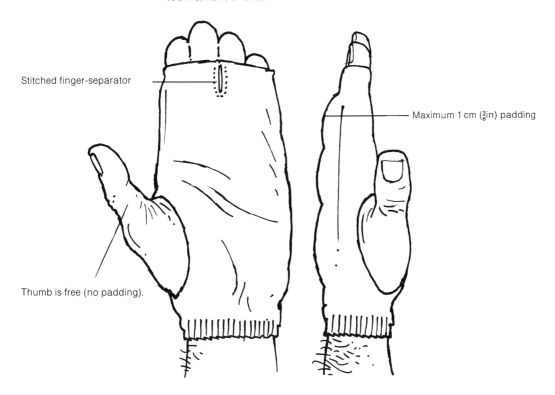

Stitched finger-separator

Maximum 1 cm ($\frac{3}{8}$in) padding

Thumb is free (no padding).

KARATE

The competition area.

It can be elevated up to 1m (3ft) above the floor area but, if it is, there must be a safety area of at least 2m (6ft 6in) around the perimeter.

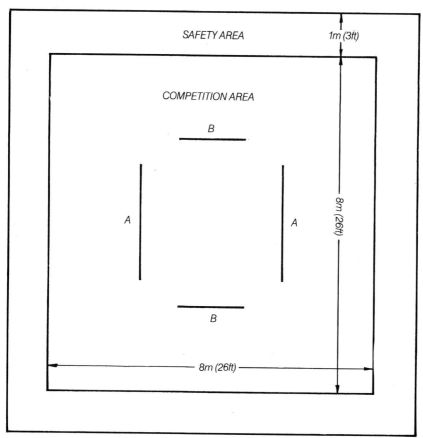

SAFETY AREA

1m (3ft)

COMPETITION AREA

B

A

A

8m (26ft)

B

8m (26ft)

A: COMPETITOR'S LINES
B: REFEREE'S/JUDGE'S LINES

The actual contest area should measure 8m (26ft) by 8m (26ft), and be made up of smaller mats. It is essential that a referee makes sure the mats do not separate during a contest because gaps can cause serious injury.

A 1m (3ft) safety area surrounds the 8m (26ft) contest area, and two markers at the centre of the area indicate where the fighters should take up position at the start, or re-start, of a contest. Fighters stand 2m (6ft 6in) apart at address. There should be no pillars, advertising hordings, walls, or anything likely to be an obstacle, within 1 m (3ft) of the outer perimeter of the fighting area.

So that's karate equipment. As you can see it does not take a lot to get a contest under way. But to perfect the art takes many years of dedication and practise. You will also have to familiarize yourself with the numerous terms which are associated with karate, most of which have Japanese origin.

TERMINOLOGY

The following are a selection of terms that will crop up quite a lot when you are participating, whether it be in a contest or during practise.

Age zuki   An uppercut type blow.

Ai-uchi   The referee's call to indicate a simultaneous score which results in no points being awarded.

Aka   The fighter designated the red belt in a *kumite*.

Ashi-barai   A leg sweep.

Ashikubi   Used in reference to the ankle or kicks made with the ankle.

Ashi-no-achi-kata   The ways of positioning the feet in readiness for an attacking or defensive move.

Ashiwaza   Leg and foot techniques as used in kicking.

Atemi   The vital points of the body.

Atoshi-baraku   Audible call from the timekeeper to indicate 'a little more time left'. Normally given by the sounding of a bell or buzzer with 30 seconds remaining.

Awasette-ippon   The score of two *waza-aris* added together to make one *ippon*.

Chakugan   The correct focus of attention in a *kata*.

Choku zuki   A direct thrust or blow.

Chudan   The mid section of the body, one of the key target areas.

Chudan-mawashi-geri   The roundhouse kick.

Chusoku   Contact point – the ball of the foot.

Dachi   Stance.

Dan   A graduate *karateka*. In other words, a senior fighter.

Dojo   Karate club or training hall.

Encho-sen   An extension to a karate contest, started with the referee calling '*shobu hajime*'.

Fudotachi   A posture adopted by the *karateka* with feet wide apart, knees bent, and in a sideways position to the opponent.

Fukushin   The judge in a *kumite* (contest).

Fumikeri   A stamping or slicing sideways kick.

Gargu-kamae   Known as the 'Reclining Dragon' stance. Vital parts of the body are protected by turning away from the opponent.

Gedan   The lower part of the trunk.

Gedan Barai   A lower sweeping block.

Geri   A kick.

Gyaku-zuki   The reverse punch.

Haisoku   Contact point – the instep.

Hajime   The referee's call to 'begin'.

Hansoku   Loss of a contest by a disqualification.

Hansoku-chui   A penalty resulting in your opponent being awarded an *ippon*.

Hantei   The referee's consultation with the judge about a decision.

KARATE

Hanteigachi A win by a decision.

Haraite A sweeping hand method of defence against an attack by your opponent's hand or foot.

Hiraken Contact point – the half-clenched fist. The contact points are the second joints of the index and middle fingers.

Hikiwake A drawn contest.

Hitosashiyubi-ipponken Contact point – the knuckle joint of the index finger.

Hiza The knee.

Hizagashira The knee-cap.

Hiza-geri An attack made with the knee cap.

Hizatsui An attack on the vital parts of your opponent's body with the knee-cap.

Ibuki A method of breathing involving the tensing of all muscles after inhaling.

Ippon A full point which is the highest score in karate. The referee will award it if a blow is delivered to one of the defined areas of the opponent's body with the correct posture and stance, from the correct distance, and with spirit and good focus.

Jion A stance position with feet apart and centre of gravity low.

Jiu-kumite Freestyle fighting.

Jodan The head area.

Jodanzuki Front punch always made to the head area.

Jogai Exit from the fighting area.

Kakato Contact point – the heel.

Kakato-geri A kick with the heel.

Kakiwake A defensive action using a thrusting hand to sweep away an opponent's wrist.

Kansa The arbitrator in a *kumite* (contest).

Karategi The karate suit. Often referred to as the '*gi*'.

Karateka A person who practises karate.

Kata A fixed sequence of training exercises which incorporate aspects of attack and defence and takes the form of imaginary fighting.

Keiko Contact point – the fingertips and thumb.

Keikoku A penalty award of a *waza-ari* to the non-offending fighter.

Kekomi A thrusting kick.

Keriage An upwards kick using either the sole of the foot or front of the ankle.

Keriwaza Kicking techniques.

Kiai The shout given out by the *karateka* as he makes impact with his opponent. The cry comes from the lower diaphragm.

Kihon Basic technical training and fighting forms.

Kizami-zuki Front hand jab.

Koken Contact point – the wrist.

Kokutsodachi One of the basic stances adopted by the *karateka*.

Kote The forearm.

Kumite A contest or match.

Kyoshi   A very high master, normally somebody of 6th, 7th or 8th Dan.

Kyu   A student.

Mae-geri   The front kick.

Makiwara   A padded board or bag used for punching and kicking training exercises.

Mawashi-geri   The roundhouse or turning kick.

Mawashi-zuki   Roundhouse punch.

Moto-no-ichi   The call for the contestants, referee and judge to return to their respective standing lines.

Mubobi   When one, or both, fighters displays a lack of regard for his own safety.

Nakayubi-ipponken   Contact point – the second joint of the middle finger.

Neko-ashi-dachi   Known as the 'Cat' stance. Most of the bodyweight is on the back foot with the right foot ready in a kicking position.

Nidan   A 2nd Dan.

Nukite   Contact point – the fingertips or spearhand.

Obi   Another name for the coloured belt worn by karateka.

Rei   The traditional bow by each *karateka* to each other before and after a contest.

Renshi   Senior expert grades, normally applied to 4th or 5th Dans . *Renshi* grade *karateka* are entitled to be called *sensei* (honourable teacher) by their juniors.

Sagi-ashidachi   Known as the 'Heron Leg' posture because the *karateka* raises one leg to a position approximately level with the knee of the supporting leg.

Sanbon   The scoring of three *ippons* in a bout.

Sandan   A 3rd Dan.

Seiken   Contact point – the fist.

Semete   An attacking fighter in *kata*.

Sensei   A term of respect from a junior to a *renshi*. It means 'honourable teacher'.

Seremade   The referee's call to indicate the contest is over. 'Time is up.'

Shihan   A term of respect by a junior for a *karateka* of 8th Dan or higher. It means 'honourable professor'.

Shikkaku   Disqualification from a bout, match and competition for a serious breach of karate rules and/or regulations.

Shiro   The wearer of the white belt in a *kumite* (contest).

Shitei   The compulsory section of a *kata* competition.

Shobu   A kumite bout.

Shodan   A 1st Dan.

Shotei   Contact point – the heel of the palm.

Shugo   The beckoning of the judge by the referee.

Shushin   The referee.

Shuto   Contact point – the knife hand.

Sokuto   Contact point – the knife foot.

KARATE

Sukuite A scooping-hand, defensive technique in which you grasp your opponent's hand, leg or foot.

Tamashiwara The art of wood-breaking.

Te The hand.

Tegatana The handsword technique effected with the thumb turned into the palm and the fingers extended. The contact point is the bottom edge of the palm.

Tekubi The wrist.

Tetsui Contact point – the fist edge.

Tewaza Hand technique.

Tobigeri A spectacular jumping kick with both feet making the opponent uncertain with which foot the kick will be made.

Tokui The free selection part of a *kata* competition.

Torimasen Call by the referee to indicate an unacceptable scoring technique.

Tsuki or **Zuki** A punch made with the hand.

Tsuzukete hajime The referee's call to 'fight on' after an interruption.

Ude The arm.

Uke A defensive action or block.

Uraken Contact point – the inverted (or back) fist.

Ushiro-geri The back kick which is made with the base of the heel.

Ushiro-mawashi-geri A reverse roundhouse kick.

Waza-ari A half-point score awarded for (a) a well-timed punch which is slightly off-centre; (b) an accurate punch which is weak, or (c) a punch slightly off target but which catches your opponent unguarded.

Yame! Referee's call to 'stop'.

Yoi Referee's call of 'ready'.

Yoko-geri A side kick.

Zanshin The state of continued commitment after a technique has landed. In other words, the fighter must be ready for a potential counter attack from his opponent.

Zenkusudachi One of the basic stances adopted by a *karateka*.

Zen-no Silent meditation.

Right, that's karate equipment and terminolgy out of the way. Now it's time to look at the rules and what you are and are not allowed to do.

THE GAME – A GUIDE

The most common form of karate is a freestyle fighting known as *jiu-kumite*. The rules are basically straightforward. You have various parts of your body with which you are allowed to attack your opponent, and there are certain parts of the body designated as target areas. To score points you have to carry out a technique which, in the referee's opinion, is good enough to carry a one-point score, an *ippon* or a half-point score a *waza-ari*. What could be simpler? The target areas are clearly defined and any other parts of your opponent's anatomy are outlawed. The target areas are: head; face; upper abdomen and stomach; chest, and back (excluding shoulders).

Karate contests take place on a square mat measuring 8m (26ft) by 8m (26ft). A cross is marked at the centre of the mat. The bouts are controlled by a referee (*shushin*) and a judge (*fukushin*) who position themselves on the mat and should be opposite each other at all times. The sole decision rests with the referee who can consult his judge to make decisions. However, if he is undecided, then an arbitrator (*kansa*), who sits outside the contest area, is called upon to assist. There are also a timekeeper and scorer positioned outside the competition area.

The referee's role is to award points, take away points for fouls and to generally make sure the contest is run properly.

The two contestants wear identifying belts, normally one red (*aka*) and one white (*shiro*) at senior international level. These are worn instead of the belts a fighter wears to signify his grade.

Before a contest, the two competitors stand facing each other at the centre of the mat at a distance 2m (6ft 6in) apart and bow to each other. Upon the referee's call of *hajime* they start the contest. All calls are made in Japanese, hence the list of terms in the previous chapter.

The two fighters will spar by means of a free exchange of blows, blocks, and counter moves until one fighter gets a fully focussed blow to one of the defined target areas. If successful, it is then up to the referee to decide if such a blow is a point-scoring one.

The referee is looking for good quality technique. For a blow to score points it must have good form, good attitude from the fighter, vigour, alertness, good timing, and be made from the ideal distance. If the referee sees a good technique delivered by one fighter he will call *yame* and the two fighters will return to their positions at the centre of the mat. The referee will then announce it as an *ippon* or *waza-ari*, to the appropriate fighter, and announce the type of point-scoring technique.

KARATE

REFEREE'S · SIGNALS

Hajime *(start).*

The signal to indicate a waza-ari.

The signal to indicate an ippon.

Tsuzukete hajime *(resume fighting).*

The signal to indicate a Keikoku, *a warning
with a* waza-ari *penalty.*

The signal to indicate shugo, the calling of the judge.

The signal to indicate a Hansoku-chui, a warning with an ippon penalty.

The signal to indicate a foul.

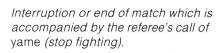

Interruption or end of match which is accompanied by the referee's call of yame (stop fighting).

(Referee's signals are continued over the page)

KARATE

The signal to indicate hikiwake *(a draw)*.

If a technique is a non-scoring one, the referee will announce torimasen *and make the above signals.*

The signal to indicate a warning with an ippon *penalty.*

The signal to indicate ai-uchi *a simultaneous technique from both fighters.*

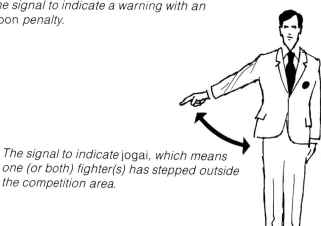

The signal to indicate jogai, *which means one (or both) fighter(s) has stepped outside the competition area.*

A fairly obvious signal indicating that a fighter is receiving his 'marching orders'. In other words, a disqualification.

An **ippon** is a full point and is the maximum single score. To be awarded, the technique must hit the target area and be perfectly executed. It must also take the opponent by surprise. This is one of the secrets of successful karate, being able to catch your opponent unaware. A score of three *ippons* wins a bout.

If, in the referee's opinion the technique was good, but not good enough to warrant an *ippon* he will call a **waza-ari**, known as the half-point. It is normally awarded for a technique that hits the target area but has been partially blocked or not carried out with the perfection of the *ippon*. While a *waza-ari* is equivalent to 50 per cent of an *ippon* in terms of scoring, it is in fact equivalent to 90 per cent of an *ippon* in technical terms. So don't expect to get awarded a *waza-ari* for a half-perfected *ippon*.

When awarding points, the referee will be looking for *zanshin*, the part of a technique often missed or ignored when carrying out a move. *Zanshin* is the state of continued commitment which continues after the technique has landed and should show the fighter maintaining concentration and awareness of the opponent's ability to counter-attack.

Penalty points are awarded for a wide variety of offences. A fighter must not step out of the competition area. If he does, then the referee will call *jogai* to indicate a warning. If he steps out of the area a second time, a half-point penalty is awarded against him. If it happens again, a full point penalty is awarded and a fourth offence results in disqualification.

But the most common penalty points are those for illegal contacts. Kicks to the eyes, knees or groin are totally outlawed. Other areas of the body can be contacted with the hands or feet but must not be made with excessive force. Once you have found your way through your opponent's defence then you should hold back on the blow or kick. Striking your opponent with excessive force will carry penalty points.

The following is a list of prohibited

Waza-ari   Ippon   Tarimasen   Mienai
                                  (no score)   *(I didn't see)*

behaviour as laid down in the rules of karate:

    a. Techniques which make contact with the throat.

    b. Techniques which make excessive contact.

    c. Attacks to the groin, joints, or instep.

    d. Attacks to the face with an open hand technique.

    e. Dangerous throws which will prevent your opponent from landing safely.

    f. Techniques which, by their nature, cannot be controlled for the safety of your opponent .

    g. Repeated direct attacks on your opponent's arms or legs.

    h. Repeated exits from the competition area (as outlined already).

    i. Grappling, wrestling, or violently pushing your opponent deliberately.

    j. Any ungentlemanly behaviour.

    k. Displaying a lack of regard for your own safety (known as *mubobi*).

    l. Feigning injury in order to gain an advantage.

Following any infringement, the referee will either give a warning or award a penalty. The following scale of penalties will be awarded by the referee:

Keikoku Awarded for minor infractions for which a warning has already been given or for offences not serious enough to warrant a *hansoku-chui.* When awarding a *keikoku* a *waza-ari* is added to your opponent's score.

Technique short of target

Technique missed target

Hikiwake *(draw)*

Hansoku-chui   If this penalty is awarded against you, your opponent is credited with an *ippon*. It is normally awarded if a *keikoku* has already been awarded in the same bout.

Hansoku   The penalty awarded for a very serious breach of the rules and results in disqualification. The opponent's score is automatically raised to *sanbon* and he becomes the winner.

Shikkaku   Disqualification from the entire tournament, competition or match following a very serious breach of the rules. The opponent's score will be raised to *sanbon*. Here are some reasons for the awarding of a *shikkaku*: (a) harming the prestige and honour of karate; (b) failing to obey the referee's orders; (c) deliberately violating the rules regarding prohibited behaviour; (d) jeapordising the smooth-running of a bout because of bad behaviour.

Because of the loose nature of the '*gi*' it is sometimes impossible, or certainly very difficult, for a referee to see whether the contact was excessive or not. On the other hand, there are some fighters who will exploit such a situation and feign injury so as to try and fool the referee into believing the blow was excessive. This is when you have to ask yourself whether you would fancy being a karate referee. The answer is probably no. His job is certainly a tough one so please, accept his decision no matter whether you believe it to be right or wrong.

KARATE

Warning   Keikoku   Hansoku-chui   Hansoku *(foul)*
(*half-point penalty*)   (*full point penalty*)

The length of a contest can vary according to the type of competition. But at senior level a men's contest will last 3 minutes while a women's or junior contest lasts 2 minutes. In certain circumstances contests can be extended to 5 minutes duration, if the rules of the competition permit. The contest will end before then if one fighter has reached the required number of points, normally three. At the end of the contest the referee will order the two fighters back to their starting lines. He will take up his position and raise his hand on the side of the winner and announce *shiro* (or *aka*) *no kachi*. The bout is ended at this point.

In major international competitions fighters normally have to endure a series of elimination bouts on a straight knock-out basis until there are just two fighters left to contest the final.

Contests can go into extra-time to decide a winner, again that depends on the rules of the competition.

Contests take place between fighters within weight categories at senior level. The weight divisions are as follows:

Men

Lightweight	– under 60kg
Super-lightweight	– under 65kg
Light-middleweight	– under 70kg
Middleweight	– under 75kg
Light-heavyweight	– under 80kg
Heavyweight	– over 80kg
Open class	– any

Women

Lightweight	– under 53kg
Middleweight	– under 60kg
Heavyweight	– over 60kg

Jogai *(exit from contest area)*   Aiuchi *(simultaneous score)*   *Excessive contact*

Now let's look at the rules of **kata**, the other most popular form of karate.

Kata is a fixed sequence of basic defence and attack routines carried out without the aid of an opponent. It is designed for practice and takes the form of fighting imaginary attackers approaching from different directions. This form of 'practice' is played at competition level where a technically good routine is crucial. An experienced judge will readily see any flaw in the *karateka*'s technique.

We will be looking at *kata* techniques later, but here are the rules affecting *kata* competitions.

First, a *kata* competition can be performed on a mat, but a polished wooden surface is better. It must obviously be free of splinters. There is no defined size of the area but it must

be large enough to enable the *karateka* to carry out his routine. Dress is the standard *karategi* and the contestant wears his appropriate belt.

Competitions take the form of individual or team matches. In team events, three fighters constitute one team which must be either all male or all female. There are no mixed teams. Each contestant is required to perform a compulsory (*shitei*) routine and a free selection (*tokui*).

A total of five judges will be designated for each match and they will be assisted by score-keepers and announcers.

A *kata* match is carried out on an elimination basis and after the first round of sequences the number of competitors is reduced to sixteen. After the second round it is reduced further to eight and the third round decides the final placings. If the same judges have officiated in all the rounds, the scores in all the rounds are aggregated. If a new set of judges is appointed for the final round, then only the points gained in the final round are counted. Each judge awards points for individual performances and displays the points allocated by holding up a card in his right hand. The maximum and minimum scores are not counted.

The judges are looking for the following points when making their assessment of a good routine:

a. It must be performed with competence and demonstrate a full understanding of the principle it contains

b. It must contain correct focus of attention, use of power, good balance, and proper breathing

c. The performance should also be evaluated with a view to discerning other points

Upon being called, the contestant will go directly to the competition area, stand on the designated line and bow to the judges. He will then announce clearly the *kata* he intends performing and start. On completion of the routine he will return to his mark and await the scoring. Upon completion of the routine the referee will call for a decision from the judges by blowing a whistle, at which point they will raise their appropriate scorecards.

There are one or two other questions that we may have left unanswered so the following chapter sets out to clear up those unanswered queries that will crop up from time to time.

Karate is not just about punching and kicking. The sparring at the beginning of a bout is very important as both fighters look for their first opening.

RULES
CLINIC

When does the timing of a contest begin?

From the moment the referee gives the call to start, *hajime*. The clock stops each time he calls *yame*.

If the rules of a contest say the first to score three points is the winner of the bout can a fighter score his three points by obtaining six **waza-aris** *(half points)*?

Yes.

Is it possible to have a tied bout?

Yes. If neither fighter is ahead on points and the officials cannot decide the winner then the bout is a tie. Normally, an extra period of time (two minutes) will be allowed to find a winner. This is called *encho-sen*. The referee will commence this extra period with the call '*shobu-hajime*'.

What happens if the scores are level at the end of, say, two minutes?

If the rules of the competition permit, 'extra-time' will be allowed and continue until the first score is made. If it were a penalty this would mean the guilty fighter would lose the contest. If the rules do not allow for an *encho-sen* the

referee will award the contest to the fighter who he feels showed superiority based on his skill of technique, fighting spirit, and a good attitude.

How many **karateka** *normally take part in team matches?*

Normally five, plus two reserves. There must be an odd number of fighters in each team.

If a bout goes into **encho-sen** *do any penalties from the original part of the bout get deleted, or are they carried forward?*

Sorry, but they're carried forward, because *encho-sen* is a continuation of the bout.

How is a team contest scored?

The number of victories is taken into consideration, and drawn matches remain drawn. The team with the most victories shall be deemed the victors. However, if they are level then points won by all fighters are accumulated and the team with the most points wins. Again, if the two teams are still level then a deciding bout will be held and the first fighter to be awarded an *ippon* or *waza-ari* shall win the match for his team. If they are

KARATE

still level after three minutes fighting an extension (*encho-sen*) will be allowed. If they are then still level, the officials will announce a winner based on the number of good techniques delivered and fighting spirit.

If both fighters land a blow simultaneously which one scores the point(s)?

Neither. They cancel each other out and the referee will call *ai-iuchi*, which means 'simultaneous'.

If a scoring technique is delivered at the same time as the end of the bout is signalled, does it still score?

Yes. However, if it is delivered *after* time has been called it shall not score and may result in a penalty being called.

You have said that the throat, groin, instep, etc are forbidden contact areas. But what happens if I make contact with, say my opponent's throat, as a result of him unbalancing himself and falling on to me?

Naturally you will not be penalized.

Likewise, if I am propelled out of the fighting area by my opponent, does this count as a jogai against me?

Again, no.

if a fighter has so many hansoku-chuis and keikokus against him that add up to a sanbon is he disqualified?

Yes. He will have *hansoku* called against him.

If a contest is interrupted before the end of its duration, is time allowed for this stoppage?

Yes. The clock is stopped the moment the contest is halted.

Are fully focussed contact blows of any description permitted?

Yes, just one – the sweeping of your opponent's leg to knock him to the ground. This must, however, be followed by a controlled punch or kick in order to score.

If a fighter comes into the arena incorrectly or inappropiately dressed, is he disqualified?

Not automatically. He has one minute in which to rectify the situation.

I understand you are not allowed to step outside the fighting area. But what happens if you do and deliver a point-winning technique, does it count?

Of course not.

England's Molly Samuel (left) and her opponent both attempt roundhouse kicks.

KARATE

Can a fighter still be penalized after the completion of a bout?

Yes. Penalties can be imposed by the referee at any time up to the contestants leaving the fighting area. Even after that penalties can be imposed for such things as ungentlemanly conduct, but such awards are only made by the chief referee or refereeing committee of that particular tournament.

Let's say two fighters injure each other simultaneously and neither can continue fighting, how is the outcome decided?

The fighter leading on points at the time of the stoppage shall be declared the winner. If the points are level then a decision, a *hantei*, will decide the bout.

What happens after each scoring blow?

The referee, judge and fighters return to their respective marks in the centre of the fighting area. The referee then announces either *ippon* or *waza-ari* to the appropriate fighter followed by the call of '*tsuzukete hajime*', which means, 'carry on'.

Apart from stopping the bout as a result of a point-scoring technique, when is the referee like to call 'yame' to stop the bout?

Well, it can be for any one of several reasons. The following are the most likely:

  a. When one or both fighters are out of the fighting area.
  b. When one fighter's *karategi* needs adjusting.
  c. When a fighter appears to be about to break one of the rules.
  d. When a fighter has broken the rules.
  e. When one or both fighters need medical attention.

  f. When one or both contestants fall or are thrown, and no effective technique follows.

Are there any rules about the wearing of jewellery when fighting?

Yes. You must not wear metallic or other objects which might injure your opponent or yourself. You mustn't have long fingernails either. Spectacles are also outlawed, I'm afraid, but soft contact lenses are permitted.

What happens in the event of a tie in a kata?

You remember earlier we said that the highest and lowest scores are discounted. Well, in the event of a tie then the minimum score is incorporated into a fighter's score for that round. If still level, then the maximum score is incorporated. In the event of a continued tie then the contestants must perform another *kata* of their choice.

Is it possible to be disqualified from a kata?

Yes. Disqualification follows if you interrupt or vary a routine or perform a *kata* different from the one drawn or indicated.

During a contest, a successful fighter has to perform three scheduled katas. Can he perform the same one during each round?

No. The one in round two must be different from that in the first round. But the one in the final round can be any one of his choice.

TECHNIQUE

The object of the *karateka* is to transmit muscular power of the whole body in a striking limb movement at speed to focus on a given object. To carry out such movements with maximum effect, use must be made of correct stance, breathing and timing.

The whole of the body, and in particular those bonier regions, can be used as weapons in karate. But even a single finger can be used as a powerful weapon, with lethal effect in the original days when it was used as an effective form of fighting. A single finger suitably strengthened would have a similar effect to that of a dagger or sword.

Don't take up karate if your sole reason is to be the next Bruce Lee. But do take it up if you want to enjoy a pleasurable and disciplined form of unarmed combat.

At an early stage of your development you need to concentrate your efforts on performing a *kata*. There is no sense in thinking you can progress into freestyle fighting (*kumite*) without being able to execute movements in the *kata*. Initially, your *kata*(s) will be slow, but you will gradually build up pace as you get more experienced.

Before we go into the various techniques we ought to reiterate that karate is about more than just scoring successful punches or kicks to various parts of your opponent's body. 'Good form' is a phrase that is crucial to good and effective karate. The technique has to be carried out with maximum effect within the framework of karate concepts and ideals. Correct **attitude** is one such component of 'good form'. Too many people take up karate with an over-eager and aggressive attitude but karate is not meant for those people. Your attitude should be of the non-malicious kind and great concentration is required in making sure that your scoring techniques do not harm your opponent.

Another characteristic of 'good form' is the **vigorous application** which defines the power and speed of the technique coupled with the insatiable desire to succeed with the technique.

And the final component of 'good form' is *zanshin*, **the state of total awareness**, even after the execution of a scoring technique. The *karateka* should always be aware of counter attacks. That is where good *zanshin* is called for.

Correct **timing** should also be considered when attempting a scoring punch or kick. To be timed correctly it must be executed so that it would have the greatest potential effort if it made contact with your opponent. Likewise the technique should be executed from a proper distance so that any punch, blow or kick will have the maximum effect. If you deliver a blow to an opponent who is moving away from you then it would not have the maximum effect and would therefore not warrant the awarding of an *ippon*.

Before moving on to specific types of technique, it is important to look at training techniques.

Most good *dojos* will have *makiwara* (padded boards) for practising and developing kicking and punching techniques. They will also help toughen the contact points. Other standard training equipment will include

KARATE

Makiwara *training boards are padded and ideal for practising kicking and punching techniques.*

Suspended punch bags are also useful aids for practising kicking and punching.

· 34 ·

TECHNIQUE

dumb bells for carrying out weight training exercises, punch bags and specially weighted leg clamps for developing leg muscles. A container of sand or polystyrene balls is useful for practising driving techniques with the hands.

The basic training, comprising blocks, strikes and kicks, and on stance, balance,

breathing, and focus, is called *kihon*. It may be practised on your own or in groups. The latter is more enjoyable. When practised in groups, the instructor or the senior grade will lead the group, encouraging them by example and by shouting commands to the rhythm of the practice.

The Zen-kutsu-dachi *stance from the side . . .*

. . . and how it looks to your opponent.

The reclining dragon stance from the side...

...and from the front.

PREPARATION

The first thing to learn is how to stand properly, so now we will look at the different stances. But before moving on to the techniques, we will look at the basic preparations for karate which it is essential to know about: generating power, breathing and being aware of warming up.

Stances

The various stances are designed for specific purposes. Those with a low centre of gravity and a wide foot stance are ideal for powerful punching, whereas others are designed for mobility and speed of technique. You should have a sound knowledge of the basic stances, and not just

The cat stance. Note how the front foot is ready to pounce or kick forward.

rely on one in particular.

The *Zen-kutsu* is one of those stances ideal for powerful punching. The centre of gravity is low, the feet are apart and the body is very stable. The arms give the impression that they are inviting a strike to the head but that is the false sense of security you are lulling your opponent into. The head and upper body are, in fact, well defended and the arms are in a good position for first defending and then turning into an attack.

The *Gargu-kamae* stance is better known as the 'reclining dragon'. The front of the body is turned away from the opponent and is designed to protect vital parts of the body.

In the *Neko-ashi-dachi* stance (the 'cat' stance) most of the bodyweight is transferred to the rear foot and the front foot is posed and ready for attacking with. With this stance you can rapidly change your position and posture.

Generating power

If you look at a discus thrower or shot putter you will notice how power is generated as a result of a rotating movement of the body before the throw. The *karateka* generates power in the same way. The rotary movements of the *karateka* transmit velocity and power to the striking limb whether it be the arm or leg. These movements also help to unbalance your opponent.

You can see how the turning of the hips can add more power into this kick.

Warming up exercises are important. Five minutes stretching like this will be of great benefit.

TECHNIQUE

Breathing

Part of the mental preparation of karate lies in the *karateka*'s ability to breath properly and goes back to some of Zen's principles.

The breathing patterns are designed to bring about a mental calm immediately prior to exploding into action and there are four distinct phases to each pattern:

a. Inhale through the nose until the lungs are full of air.

b. Force all the air downwards towards the diaphragm. You will not find this easy at first but after a bit of practice you will find you are transferring the air, and at the same time strengthening the muscles of the abdomen. The ability to breath in the area of the abdomen and the use of the *kiai* help generate remarkable power.

c. Exhale quietly through the nose.

d. Finally, force the last remaining air out of your lungs.

An ideal breathing exercise for karate is *ibuki*. After inhaling, tense all your muscles, particularly those in the abdomen region. Open your mouth wide and gently bite the back of your tongue. Exhale as if you are blowing a 'raspberry'. When you feel you have emitted all the air, have one last effort to push out the last drop. You will be amazed how much air you push out of your lungs.

Warming up

Don't forget to warm up when you first enter your training hall. There is nothing worse than starting any strenuous exercise from cold. Karate is certainly no different. Place some emphasis on stretching exercises to protect your muscles and improve their suppleness. Without any reasonable level of suppleness many kicks are impossible to carry out.

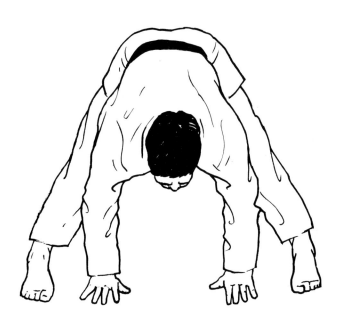

This exercise will help get your back supple and ready for karate action.

KARATE

Three more good stretching exercises.

Right, before we go on to techniques, you ought to familiarise yourself with the points of your body that are designated 'contact points', in other words, those parts which are acceptable in scoring techniques.

TECHNIQUE

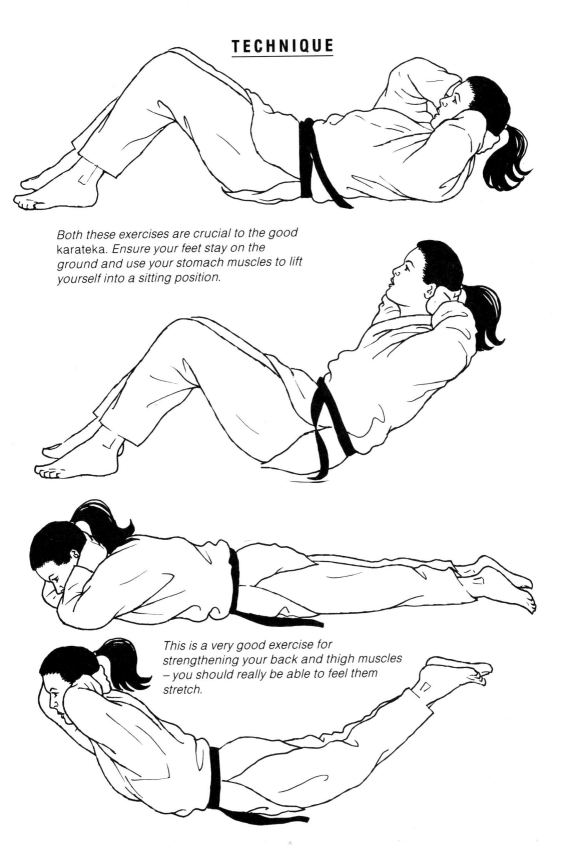

Both these exercises are crucial to the good karateka. *Ensure your feet stay on the ground and use your stomach muscles to lift yourself into a sitting position.*

This is a very good exercise for strengthening your back and thigh muscles – you should really be able to feel them stretch.

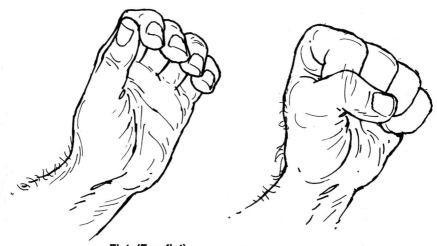

Fist (Forefist).
*To create a good forefist bend your fingers
inwards and tightly grip the first two fingers
with your thumb. Don't tuck your thumb under
the fingers.*

The contact points

The fist (Seiken)   Contact is made with the
knuckles of the first and middle fingers of the
clenched fist. Make sure the fist is well secured
because the tighter the fist, the firmer the wrist.

The back fist (Uraken)   This is employed
when striking to the side of the head. The grip
is similar to the last contact but the wrist is
slightly bent.

The knifehand (Shuto)   This part of the
hand is often used in wood-breaking. It is also
used in *kata*. Make sure your thumb
is bent inwards. As well as being a useful
attacking aid, the knifehand is also useful for
blocking.

The spearhand (Nukite)   Very useful when
attacking soft parts of your opponent's body,
like the abdomen. Again, make sure your
thumb is bent inwards. The contact point is the
middle three fingers.

The single-knuckle fist (Ippon Ken)   Only
the middle knuckle is extended and the
fingertip of your first finger is held securely.

The wrist (Koken)   The actual contact point
is that part of the lower arm between your wrist
and palm of the hand. It is used in blocks and
attacks to the face and, sometimes, stomach.
Make sure your wrist is well bent and out of
the way so you can make contact with that
boned part of the hand as outlined.

The elbow (Empi)   A versatile contact point
because you can use it to strike from any
direction; forwards, sideways, upwards and
even backwards.

Important: knifehand, spearhead, single-
knuckle fist and elbow attacks are
particularly dangerous; so much so that they
are not allowed in competition. Practise them
very carefully.

Back of the fist.
The grip of the fingers is similar to the forefist but the wrist is slightly bent this time.

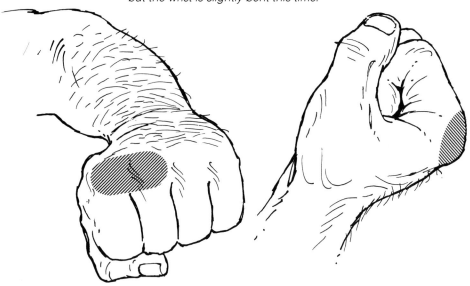

Knifehand.
A useful contact point for both blocking and attacking. It is important that you bend your thumb inwards otherwise you could sustain a nasty injury.

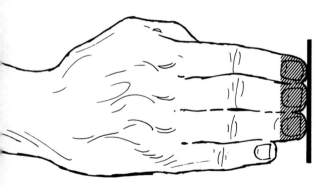

Spearhand.
An important 'weapon' when attacking those softer parts of your opponent's body. The contact is made with the tips of the three middle fingers so you will have to bend your middle finger slightly to get them in line.

Single-knuckle fist.
The fist is clenched tightly and the middle knuckle is extended.

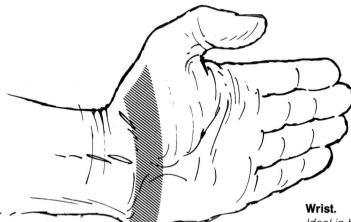

Wrist.
Ideal in blocking. The contact point is the back of the palm immediately before the wrist.

Britain's former world champion Jeoff Thompson successfully executing a back fist.

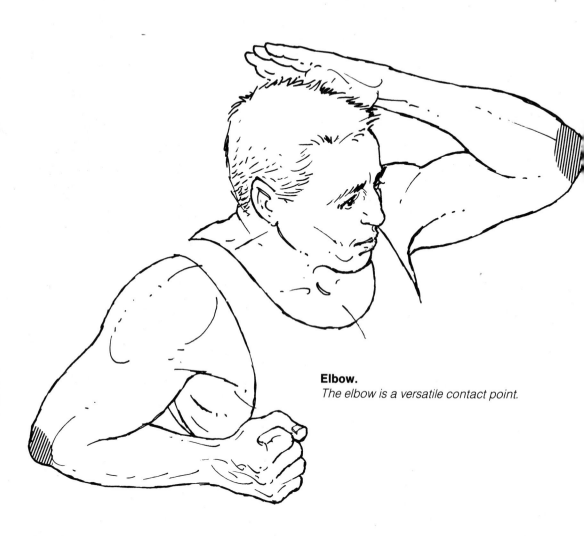

Elbow.
The elbow is a versatile contact point.

Now for the legs and feet:

The heel (Kakato)   Used for backward kicks.

The instep (Haisoku)   Used more often than not for roundhouse kicks to the head. Keep the toes pointing outwards.

The ball of the foot (Chusoku)   Also used in roundhouse kicks as well as for front kicks. Keep your toes well bent upwards.

The knife foot (Sokuto)   This contact utilizes the outside of the foot and is used mainly in sidekicks.

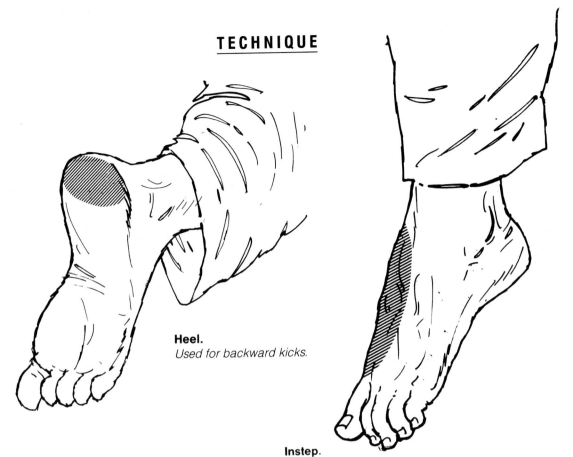

Heel.
Used for backward kicks.

Instep.
Keep the toes pointed downwards. The instep is used for roundhouse kicks.

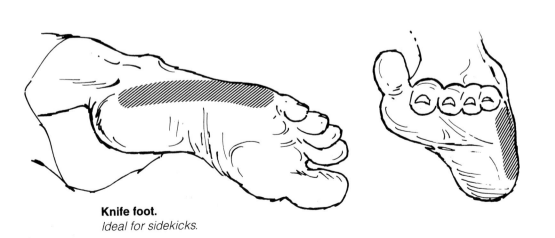

Knife foot.
Ideal for sidekicks.

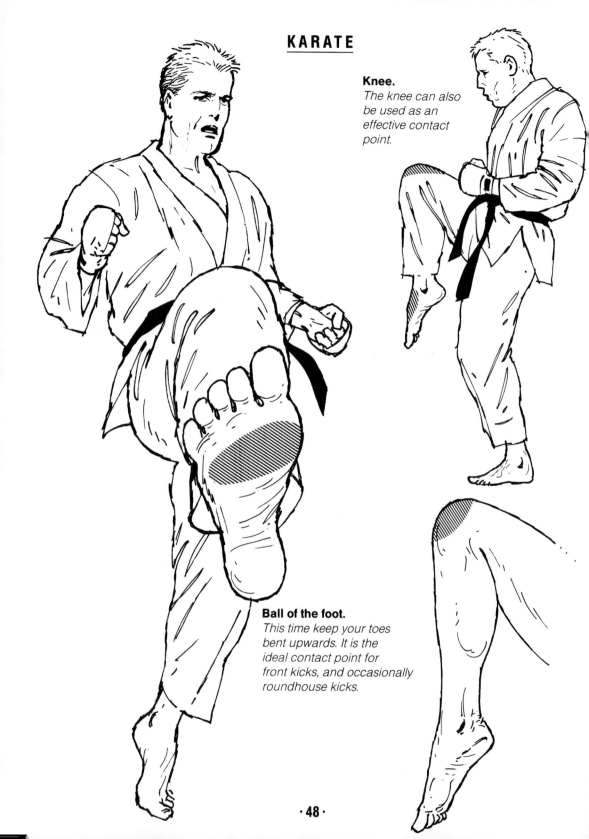

Knee.
The knee can also be used as an effective contact point.

Ball of the foot.
This time keep your toes bent upwards. It is the ideal contact point for front kicks, and occasionally roundhouse kicks.

The knee (Hiza) Yes, the knee is a useful contact point, particularly into your opponent's stomach.

Note that in a karate competition you make an attack with any open-hand technique or with the elbow or knee.

Don't forget, we have already said that almost any boney part of the body can be used as a weapon (for example the single finger). The aforementioned are the most widely used, but don't feel you are restricted to them.

TECHNIQUES

Now for some punching and kicking techniques which will be looked at from two views – those of the attacker and those of the defender. You will need to learn how to combat attacking moves as well as making them.

The first thing we must emphasize is the simplicity of karate. One fighter looks for an opening in order to attack while the other evades this attack and, if successful, attempts to build up a counter-attack. The tactical battle is the one whereby the two fighters look for that first opening.

There are three ways of attacking: **kicking. punching** and **sweeping**. But as the latter is for the more advanced fighter we are not going to give it a great deal of space in this book. Initially you will only need to learn to develop the first two skills.

Punching Unlike boxing, where the fighters are generally weaker with one hand than the other, the *karateka* needs to be an expert with both hands. If you can punch equally well with both hands then you have more chance of catching your opponent unaware. While kicking techniques look more attractive to the newcomer it cannot be emphasized too strongly that you also need to practise and develop punching techniques. And what is more, if you find that, say, your right hand is far superior to your left at punching, then you must spend time practising punching with your left hand. There is no point in practising what you are good at, is there?

Kicking The advantage of kicking over punching is the fact that you can put more space between yourself and your opponent, thus reducing the risk of a quick counter-attack. He can still counter-attack if your kick is a non-scoring one, but you will have more time to defend yourself.

Place your weight on your front foot to gain the maximum reach.

Punching techniques
The front jab (*Kizami-zuki*)

Target Area:
The face.

Attacking:
One of the basic punches, it is very little different to the jab in boxing. It is effective, if not as a scoring punch, but for opening up your opponent's defence. Speed of thrust is important, both in executing the punch and, if unsuccessful, in retreating the arm and fist.

Use of the punchbag in training is good exercise for the front punch.

Defending:
To spot the front punch coming keep an eye on your opponent. If he moves closer to you rapidly it is likely that a front punch is on its way. From your own stance position you

Britain's Jim Collins (left) the 1984 world Kumite 70kg champion.

KARATE

Your opponent will give a clue that he is about to punch by moving quickly forward.

Be alert, and sweep his attacking arm away with your left arm and be ready to attack with your right.

TECHNIQUE

should sweep with your forearm and deflect the punch. The swivelling of the hips helps with the defensive movement. But after preventing the attack, you must be ready to counter-attack, probably with your other hand.

The back fist (*Uraken*)
Target Area:
Side of the head.

Attacking:
Similar to the front punch but this time the blow is with the back of the hand. It is used more as a counter-attack and requires very quick hands to perfect.

The back fist
From a side-on position, with your elbow pointing at your opponent's face, straighten your attacking arm to carry out the successful back fist.

Countering the back fist

Note how the attacking left arm of the fighter on the right is deflected, and how the other fighter quickly attacks with a punch.

TECHNIQUE

*Rotating the hips adds extra power and speed to the
reverse punch.*

The reverse punch

Being able to move sideways is important in countering the reverse punch. Make sure your opponent's arm is deflected to the side and then quickly swivel your hips to come in with a counter attack.

Defending:
The back fist is a difficult punch to spot because you're never sure whether it is going to be a front punch or back fist. However, quick reactions are essential and if you move your head out of the way, it will bring your left upper arm upwards and ready to take the force of the punch. At the same time your opponent's middle area will be exposed and if you can recover your balance quick enough, and be alert enough, you can counter to that area.

The reverse punch (*Gyaku-zuki*)
Target Area:
Head and upper body from waist upwards, but excluding the arms and neck.

Attacking:
It is similar to the front punch but this time the damage is caused by the back hand as opposed to the front hand. The punch is made more powerful and effective by swinging your hips as you turn to make the punch. Because the fist has farther to travel than in the front punch you have to be very quick, or alternatively, make sure you have a good opening otherwise you will find the punch blocked.

Defending:
As mentioned, you will have that little bit more time to spot the reverse punch and it is easily deflected with your forearm. Again you should be ready to counter-attack.

The roundhouse strike ... *so-called because you take your opponent's attacking arm out and counter-attack with your other hand.*

Above and opposite: *The front kick is a useful kick for smaller fighters matched against taller opponents because they can get under the taller man's guard.*

The roundhouse strike (*Mawashi-zuki*)

Target Area:
Side of the face.

Attacking:
Your right fist should be either fully hidden behind your back or partly hidden by your side. You lunge forward with your left arm from the stance position and then rapidly bring forward the right fist into your opponent's face. Contact is with the forefist.

Defending:
Blocking would be similar to that for the front punch.

Kicking techniques (*Geri*)
The front kick (*Mae-geri*)

Target Area:
Stomach/upper abdomen.

Attacking:
This is the first kick you will learn. But the big mistake many novices make is in believing the contact point is the toes. It is not. The contact point is the ball of the foot. To carry out an effective front kick you must ensure that your knee is lifted high enough and your leg is then straightened to carry out the kick. It is not a sweeping kicking movement from the floor into your opponent's stomach.

KARATE

Emmanuel Pinda (left) of France. He was the
1984 Open class Kumite world champion.

TECHNIQUE

Defending and counter attacking the front kick requires
a good quick action moving from one side to the other.
The first is to deflect the attacking leg and the second
to deliver the counter attack.

Defending:
Side-step the kick and sweep the attacker's leg away with your front arm from a normal stance position. Your other arm should then be free for the counter-attack. And don't forget, you should have the advantage after a block because your opponent will be off balance.

The roundhouse kick (*Mawashi-geri*)
Target Area:
Head, stomach or back.

Attacking:
Like the front kick, the roundhouse kick depends a great deal on good swivelling of the hips. The knee should also be lifted high before execution of the kick. The roundhouse is a spectacular kick and if perfected well can get you a full point (*ippon*). The instep is used in the roundhouse kick. The ball of the foot can be used but, because it is dangerous, there is an 'unwritten' law amongst *karatekas* that says only the instep is used. The roundhouse kick to the face calls for perfect balance and your trunk should be at right angles to the standing leg. The reverse roundhouse (*Ushiro-mawashi-geri*) is made with the ball of the foot contacting your opponent's cheek bone. Like all roundhouse kicks, speed is important, and the transference of the feet from stance position to kicking position should be in one continuous movement.

Defending:
The most effective defence is by stepping forward from your normal stance and

dropping your left arm to block with, but making sure you take the force of the kick on the muscle, not the elbow. If you keep your other elbow high it gives you the opportunity to counter-attack with, say, a back fist. The block against a roundhouse kick to the face lends itself to a perfect counter-attack because your opponent will be off-balance and with his back to you. To counter a roundhouse kick to the face you must sweep your opponent's kicking leg out of the way. This will have the effect of turning him around.

'Eyeing up' an opponent before deciding on what form of attack to adopt – in this case the roundhouse kick. Note how the attacker is leaning back as he prepares to execute the kick.

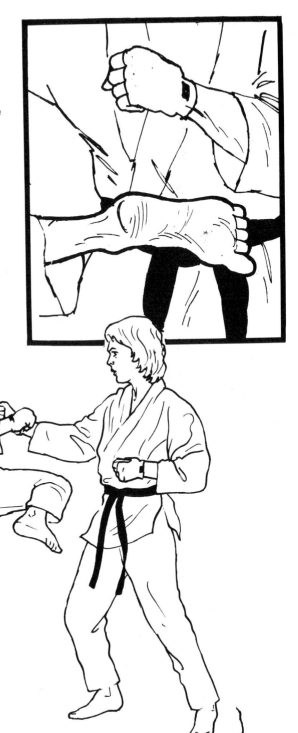

The roundhouse kick is defended by brushing aside the attacking leg of your opponent and then quickly swivelling your hips to deliver your counter punch.

Timing, and a full extension of the attacking leg are
important with the back kick.

Below and opposite: *The quick 'one-two' is employed yet again when defending the back (or side) kick. The attacking leg is brushed aside and, again, the hips are swivelled to enable the counter punch to be made.*

Back kick (*Ushiro-geri*)

Target Area:
Abdomen.

Attacking:
Regarded as the most powerful kick in karate. It is made more lethal by the turning of the body as you turn into the kick. It is effective if carried out properly but the big problem, as you can see, is the fact that you turn your back on your opponent to make the kick. If blocked, you will be in all sorts of trouble.

Defending:
Blocking is done by thrusting downwards with the front arm onto the kicking leg. The counter-attack is made quickly with the other arm.

Side kick (*Yoko-geri*)

Target Area:
Chest/stomach.

Attacking:
This time the power of the kick comes from the thrusting of the leg rather than twisting of the hips. A very high knee position is essential and the power is generated from that position as the leg is straightened. Your opponent can be confused into thinking you will be effecting a front leg roundhouse. It can be effective if your opponent is near to the edge of the competition area because, if it doesn't score you a point it may well carry a penalty for him if he steps off the mat.

Defending:
The kick is defended against in the same way as the back kick.

Those are the fundamental punches and kicks which you should try and develop. Don't forget, you will be penalized if they are carried out with too much force. And remember, one of the keys to successful karate is being able to hold back on the punch or kick after getting through your opponent's defence.

Next we will look a bit closer at **blocking** because it is a very useful part of the *karateka's* repertoire. Good blocking will prevent a successful attack from your opponent and at the same time set up a counter-attack from you. Many top international fighters are expert counter-attackers, letting their opponent do the work to begin with.

Timing, balance, and keeping an eye on your opponent are three vital ingredients with the side kick. But you must also execute it correctly, and a very high knee position at the start of the move is important.

Cross-blocking techniques are rarely seen at competitive level but are still a useful form of defence.

Blocking usually takes two forms. It can either be a blow to an attacking limb, or a simple deflection. As a golden rule, punches to the head should be deflected upwards, those to the body should be deflected sideways, and those to the groin area should be deflected downwards.

In addition to the single arm blocks as outlined in the techniques already described there are two-handed cross blocks with, as the name implies, the arms crossed. They are used as a defence of the face.

From a forward stance the forearm block is very effective and with a sweeping movement of the right arm blocks your opponent's attack.

The downward block is ideal against kicks or punches to the stomach or abdomen region.

One of the leading female karate exponents, Helen Raye.

KARATE

When taking part in *kumite* fighting you will find it essential to string together a series of attacks, blocks, counter-attacks, and so on. This is where a good *kata* comes in useful as you put together a series of combination moves which will all go towards making you a better fighter. However, you must always remember that there is a good chance your attacking punch or kick will be blocked. Unless you are ready with your contingency attack then you will lose the advantage. So, be alert at all times. No matter what discipline you are carrying out you must always learn to keep your eyes on your opponent at all times and remember a good strong *kiai* (shout) counts towards winning points.

Finally, a brief mention of *tamashiwara* (woodbreaking), the spectacular aspect of karate and the one which many uninitiated believe is the only form of karate. In truth, very few *karateka* practice woodbreaking. However, its practice takes in the most widely taught of karate's principles: **empty the mind of all thoughts**.

Tamashiwara is, in effect, the combination of everything the *karateka* has already learned; discipline and strength. Unlike *kata* and *kumite*, where the *karateka* cannot display his feats of strength, *tamashiwara* gives the opportunity to show all of his skills. But many regard this branch of karate as the showmanship side of the sport.

The striking parts of the body used in *tamashiwara* require tremendous strength and power, but this power can only be obtained once the fear of striking something hard has gone. That is the spiritual aspect of karate. For the time being forget about *tamashiwara* and concentrate on your kata and punching and kicking techniques.

We have already mentioned the **kata** and it is important that you use this as your starting point. All *katas* commence with a defensive move followed invariably by an attacking move. In some instances the defensive and attacking moves are similar and thus are designed to confuse your opponent when involved in a *kumite* contest.

Opposite: An example of a combination of a front kick and a front punch. The former has been blocked but on regaining balance the front punch has been employed.

TECHNIQUE

We hope we have given you a firm basis for getting started in karate. And as we have said in every book in the *Play the Game* series, we cannot turn you into a champion, only **you** can do that. And the only way you can develop is by practising regularly, and by listening to and taking advice from more senior fighters. If you do, then you will spend many happy years enjoying one of the finest and most disciplined of all martial arts.

The back fist/back leg roundhouse combination. Again the latter is employed after the backfist has been blocked.

Until her recent retirement Japan's Mie Nakayama was the leading women's Kata fighter and was world champion three times.

USEFUL
ADDRESSES

Martial Arts Commission
Broadway House
15–16 Deptford Broadway
London SE8 4PE
Tel: 081 691 8711

World Union of Karate-do Organizations
Senpaku Sinko Building
1–15–16 Toranoman
Minatu-Ku
Tokyo 105
Tel: 010–81–3–5036638
or:
122 Rue de la Tombe Issoire
75014 Paris
France
Tel: 010 33(1)
43 95 42 00

English Karate Governing Body
12 Princes Avenue
Woodford Green
Essex
IG8 0ZN
Tel: 081 504 4455

Scottish Karate Board of Control
48 Ryde Road
Wishaw
Scotland NL2 7DX
Tel: 0698 357322

Northern Ireland Karate Board
House of Sport
Upper Malone Road
Belfast BT9 5LA
Tel: 0232 381222

Welsh Karate Federation
Smalldrink
Parsonage Lane
Begelly
Kilgetty
Dyfed
Tel: 0834 813776

Current World Open Champion Wayne Otto in devastating form

RULES CLINIC

INDEX

Britain's best known karate champion, Team Coach David Donovan O.B.E., coaches great new talent Molly Samuel.

INDEX